W9-BIW-021

DATE DUE		

Authors
Kids Love

Christopher Paul Curtis

An Author Kids Love

by Michelle Parker-Rock

Enslow Elementary

an imprint of

Enslow Publishers, Inc.

40 Industrial Road
Box 398
Berkeley Heights, NJ 07922
USA

http://www.enslow.com

This book is based on a live interview with Christopher Paul Curtis
on September 11, 2007.

*For Barack Obama and his historical presidency,
and for C.P.C. and his wonderful historical fiction.
Thanks—with respect and admiration for all your accomplishments.*

Library of Congress Cataloging-in-Publication Data

Parker-Rock, Michelle.
    Christopher Paul Curtis : an author kids love / Michelle Parker-Rock.
        p. cm.— (Authors kids love)
    Includes bibliographical references and index.
    Summary: "A biography of Christopher Paul Curtis based on a one-on-one interview between Curtis and the author"—Provided by publisher.
    ISBN-13: 978-0-7660-3161-6
    ISBN-10: 0-7660-3161-6
    1. Curtis, Christopher Paul—Juvenile literature. 2. Authors, American—20th century—Biography—Juvenile literature. 3. African American authors—Biography—Juvenile literature. 4. Curtis, Christopher Paul—Interviews—Juvenile literature. 5. African American authors—Interviews—Juvenile literature. 6. Children's stories—Authorship—Juvenile literature. I. Title.
    PS3553.U6944Z83 2009
    813'.54—dc22
    [B]   2009022379

Printed in the United States of America

10 9 8 7 6 5 4 3 2 1

To Our Readers: We have done our best to make sure that all Internet addresses in this book were active and appropriate when we went to press. However, the author and publisher have no control over and assume no liability for the material available on those Internet sites or on other Web sites they may link to. Any comments or suggestions can be sent by e-mail to comments@enslow.com or to the address on the back cover.

♻ Enslow Publishers, Inc., is committed to printing our books on recycled paper. The paper in every book contains 10% to 30% post-consumer waste (PCW). The cover board on the outside of each book contains 100% PCW. Our goal is to do our part to help young people and the environment too!

Photo Credits: Courtesy of Christopher Paul Curtis, pp. 3 (top and middle), 10, 12, 15, 17, 20, 23, 26, 29; Michelle Parker-Rock © 2007, pp. 1, 3 (bottom), 6, 39, 43; Random House, Inc., pp. 33, 45.

Cover Photos: Front cover image Michelle Parker-Rock © 2007; back cover image courtesy of Christopher Paul Curtis.

Contents

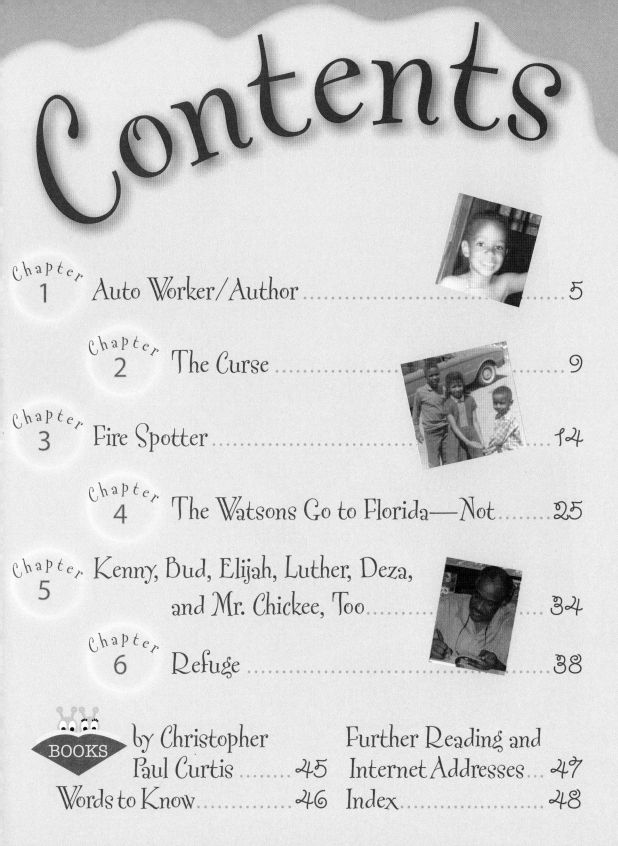

Auto Worker/ Author

Christopher Paul Curtis was forty-two years old in 1995 when his first book, *The Watsons Go to Birmingham—1963*, was published. He had taken a year off from his job at a warehouse to write a story about a ten-year-old boy named Kenny and his family during the 1960s. "I didn't even tell people about the book," he said. "I thought maybe my mother and a couple of my siblings might buy it, but that's all."

Much to Curtis's surprise, *The Watsons* was named a Newbery Honor book and a Coretta Scott King Author Honor Book in 1996. He found himself catapulted into a new and unexpected life. "It was a whole different world," he said. "Everything changed."

Four years later, Curtis became the first African-American man to receive a Newbery Medal, which was given for his novel *Bud, Not Buddy*. The book also won the Coretta Scott King Author Award, making him the first person to win both awards at the same time. Then in 2008, Curtis won another

Some of Christopher Paul Curtis's collection of books, music, model cars, and awards he's won

Coretta Scott King Author Award and a Newbery Honor for *Elijah of Buxton*. He said:

> A writer spends a lot of time alone while he is writing, and he does not get a lot of feedback during the process. In addition, there are not a lot of black voices in children's literature, although there are more than before. Therefore, when I, or any African-American author, receive recognition, it holds a special feeling. These awards are significant to me because they recognize that I'm doing something well and that others are proud of me. Pats on the back are good. However, to me, the highest praise comes when a young reader tells me, "I really liked your book." The young seem to be able to say "really" with a clarity, a faith, and an honesty that we as adults have long forgotten. That is why I write.

Although he is pleased with this success, Curtis is grateful that it did not come to him early in life. He said:

> I think I can see how, if it happens to you when you're young, you might think that this is either something you deserve or that this is the way things are going to be. But when you become successful in your forties, you have a different

Awards and Medals

The Newbery Medal is a prestigious literary prize that is given each year to an author for his or her important contribution to American literature for children. The Newbery Honor is given to praiseworthy runners-up. The Coretta Scott King Award acknowledges excellence by African-American writers. One Author Award is given annually. The Coretta Scott King Honor recognizes books in second place.

perspective than when you are younger. You look at it as it is here now, but it could be gone tomorrow.

Curtis said he still feels the lasting effects of his thirteen years in the Fisher Body Automobile Plant #1 in Flint, Michigan, where he worked on an assembly line hanging eighty-pound car doors on Buicks. It was the first serious job that he had, and although he hated it from the first minute he started there until the day he quit, it made quite an impression on him. "So much," he said, "that now, I see myself as an auto worker/author."

The Curse

Christopher Paul Curtis was born in Flint, Michigan, on May 10, 1953, to Herman Elmer Curtis Jr. and Leslie Jane Lewis Curtis. His father was a chiropodist, a foot doctor. His mother attended Michigan State College in East Lansing and was the first African-American woman to live in the dormitories. She also became the first black history teacher in the Flint school system, and she helped develop the district's black history program.

Herman and Leslie Curtis had four other children, Christopher's older sister, Lindsey, and

their younger siblings, Cydney, David, and Sarah.
Curtis said:

> I was the first son, and my father wanted to
> name me Herman Elmer the third. My mother
> wouldn't allow it, and I'm always grateful to
> her for not giving me the name Herman or Elmer.
> Instead, I was named after my mother's twin
> brother, Paul, but I don't know where she got
> Christopher.

Curtis's parents were from Grand Rapids, Michigan. On the advice of Herman's father, Herman Curtis Senior, they moved to Flint in 1950. Flint's population was growing, and people there needed foot doctors.

Flint was a one-company town. The company was Fisher Body, a part of General

Christopher's parents, Herman and Leslie Curtis

Motors, which at one time was considered the major builder of auto bodies. Many of the people who moved to Flint came from the South, and some of the people in Flint were prejudiced and intolerant. "There was a lot of discrimination in the town and in the factory," said Curtis. While discrimination was not always obvious in Flint (for example, black people were not refused service in restaurants), there were places that would not hire individuals because they were black. "You would be good enough to spend your money someplace, but you couldn't work there," he said.

However, when the

Book FACT

Flint—The Vehicle City

At the end of the nineteenth century, the city of Flint was famous for making horse-drawn carriages, and it became known as "the vehicle city." Later, the carriage companies made parts for cars. In 1936, laborers shut down Fisher Body Plants #1 and #2 and staged a sit-down strike, protesting the bad working conditions. After forty-four days, General Motors and the United Auto Workers Union came to an agreement, including the right for industrial workers to organize and bargain with their employers. The strike is often called one of the most important episodes in the history of labor unions.

factory became desperate for workers, it started hiring African Americans. The first black employees were given jobs as janitors. Later on, as production increased, the company hired black people to work on the assembly line.

Herman Curtis's chiropodist practice was slow

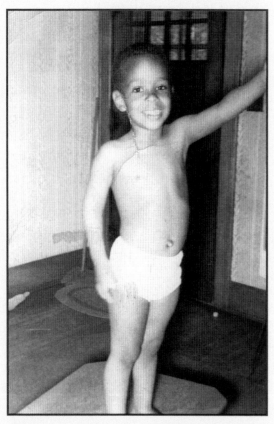

to begin with. "My mother felt the problem was that my father wouldn't charge people for his services," Curtis said. It was the days before General Motors had medical insurance for its workers, and people had to pay cash for medical care. The Curtises were middle class, but many people in their community were poor.

Christopher Paul Curtis as a little boy. He was the second of five children.

My mother said my father just wouldn't make them pay. He was not much of a businessman. For whatever reason, his practice was not a success.

12

When Christopher was born, his father took a job at a car wash to earn extra money. "That almost killed him," said Curtis. "Then he went to work at Fisher Body. He always said that I forced him into the factory because he wasn't making enough money as a chiropodist to support two kids."

Herman Curtis started out working in the metal press room.

It was a horrible place where they made the stamped metal parts, but gradually he got better and better jobs. He was the first black production foreman in the factory who was not a janitor, and eventually, he ended up with a good job as the head of education at Fisher Body.

Curtis knew that even though his parents strongly discouraged it, if nothing else worked out for him, he too could always go to the factory and get a job that paid a lot of money. "That may have been a good thing for some folks," said Curtis, "but for me it wasn't. It was a curse of my own making."

Chapter 3

Fire Spotter

"I think I was a typical kid," said Curtis. "I had my buddies, and we played football and baseball. We played with our little green plastic army men and plastic dinosaurs. There was always something going on." Curtis loved fishing, too. He got his first fishing kit from the back of a comic book for $12.95. "It had something like four thousand lures, a rod, a reel, and a knife," he said, "but I never caught a fish with that outfit. As much as I loved fishing then, I have no desire for it now."

In those days, Flint had only two TV channels. "Every once in a while you could pick up a channel from Detroit," said Curtis, "but television was not a big thing, and there were no DVDs."

Curtis was a happy kid—loved and well taken care of. "My needs were met," he said, "but my wants were not." When he asked for a bicycle, his mother said no because she thought it would be too dangerous.

> Instead, my grandmother bought me a scooter. It had two wheels, a little handle on top, and you pushed it with one foot. My cousins rode on their bikes and I rode on my scooter behind them. You can't keep up with a bike on a scooter.

Curtis also wanted a BB gun, another thing his mother disapproved of. Eventually, his younger brother David got one from somewhere. The boys

Christopher with his little brother, David

usually kept it hidden, but they would go out into the woods and shoot it. "This BB gun was so slow you could actually see the BB coming," said Curtis. "I remember one time watching the BB come at me before it hit me in the forehead."

One Christmas, Curtis was hoping to get a set of HO-scale slot cars, the kind with many yards of track that went up, down, over, and around. Unfortunately, his father did not know there were different sizes of cars. HO cars are usually three to four inches long. "On Christmas day, I remember coming down to find one slot car the size of a shoe that just went round and round on an oval track nailed to a board. I know now it's the thought that counts, but I sure wasn't impressed at the time."

On the other hand, Curtis credits his parents for giving him a big advantage. "I had all kinds of information because they would explain things and tell me how things worked." He remembers coming home from first or second grade to find a new bookcase in the hallway filled with encyclopedias. His older sister Lindsey would read the entries to him.

Christopher (at left) with Sarah, their mother, and David. Curtis says he was a "typical kid."

On Saturdays, Curtis and his siblings would go to the library with his father, who had become involved with the United Auto Workers, a labor union that protected the rights of people working in the factory. "He'd put us in the children's section, and then he'd go over to the law and labor books," said Curtis. "I remember going through the picture books and having a lot of fun. I think that's where I first realized that the library was a special place."

Curtis attended Flint city schools—Dewey Elementary from kindergarten to second grade and Clark Elementary for third through sixth grades.

Curtis thought school was interesting, and he was always excited to learn new things. "I was also competitive," he said. "We'd have tests, and I'd try to zip through them as fast as I could and slam my pencil down. I always wanted to be first with things like that."

Curtis was generally a good student, and things came easily to him. When he was in fourth grade, he told his siblings that he was going to be an author and write a book. They laughed at him. But his mother reassured him about his writing and praised him for a project he did in sixth grade:

> We were given an assignment to write a newspaper about things that were happening in Roman times. I brought it home, wrote it, and gave it to my mother to read. She said she wished I hadn't brought it home because the teacher would think that an adult did it. She felt it was that good, and it gave me tremendous encouragement. She made me believe I had a natural ability to write at an early age. I think it is so important to have someone in your corner at the beginning.

In sixth grade, Curtis was reading at a twelfth-grade level, but he did not find a lot of pleasure in books. He would read what he had to for school, but he did not read books on his own. He was, however, a big fan of *Mad Magazine* and had lots of *Superman* and *Batman* comics. Then in junior high, Curtis read *The Bridges at Toko-Ri* by James Michener. "It grabbed me," he said. "Something happened in the story and it almost made me cry. I thought it was great that a book could do that."

During third through sixth grades, Curtis's family lived in a segregated black community. In fifth and sixth grade, every Tuesday afternoon, he would walk to another school for academically talented and gifted children. He was one of just a few African-American students in the class. "I grew up in a cocoon," he said. "We were aware of racial issues, but we also had the ability to do whatever we chose to do." Curtis's parents made sure that their children were protected. "If we told them that something happened at school with a teacher, we knew that they would go up to the school to find out what occurred," he said.

In the early 1960s, Curtis's parents were involved in the civil rights movement, and his

Christopher with David and their father. Curtis's parents were both active in the civil rights movement.

family belonged to the National Association for the Advancement of Colored People and the Urban League. His father was also devoted to helping other black men learn skilled trades and get better jobs in the factory. Often this involved tutoring them for the trade skills exam, which tested a worker's knowledge of his or her craft. Curtis said:

> Many black people would take the test and get hammered by the math questions because they

never had the higher level courses in school. On Saturdays, a group of black men would come over to our house and my father would tutor them. I remember him coming home one time so happy because one of the men had gotten a perfect score. The testing board thought he had cheated, so they made him take the test again with different problems. I was aware that there were things that were racist. I even remember picketing at various restaurants with my parents when I was in grades three to eight.

Eighth grade was a turning point in Curtis's life. The neighborhood he grew up in was torn down and the city built an expressway through it. His family moved to Stonegate, a development of small townhouses. Of the 192 families that lived there, only four of the families were black. "That was a different kind of experience," he said.

Curtis went from a school that was all African-American to Whittier, a school that was about 25 percent black. The year after that, he attended McKinley, which was less than ten percent black. His brother went to a school where he was the first and only African-American child. "I don't know if

Book FACT

The NAACP and the Urban League

The National Association for the Advancement of Colored People (NAACP) is the oldest not-for-profit civil rights organization in the United States. Its purpose is to advance equal educational, political, social, and economic rights for all people; eliminate hatred, prejudice, and racial discrimination; and ensure that people of color and all ethnic minorities are given opportunities under the law to vote and be treated justly in court. The National Urban League is the oldest and largest community-based nonprofit civil rights organization in the United States. Over one hundred groups nationwide provide local programs and services on education, employment, housing, health, and leadership.

it was because we moved to a new area," said Curtis, "but I just didn't like going to school anymore. I also didn't like the kids I went to school with."

As a young boy, Curtis thought about becoming a doctor, lawyer, or professional football, baseball, or basketball player. However, in eighth or ninth grade, while he was thumbing through a box of job descriptions, he found his dream job—fire spotter.

Being away from people sounded like a pretty good job to me at that time. I would live like a hermit in a tree house in the woods and look for fires.

Participating in Suitcase Theater gave Curtis (in second row, center) the chance to travel in the United States, Canada, and even Europe.

During high school, Curtis bagged groceries at the local A&P market and mowed lawns in his neighborhood. Twice a week during his senior year, he drove to Lansing, Michigan, to rehearse with a theater troupe called Suitcase Theater. In June of 1971, he missed his high school graduation and the prom to travel with the group. "It's not like I had a date anyway," he said. For the next two months, they toured parts of Europe, Canada, and the United States, performing the poems of Langston Hughes and promoting hope and togetherness. The trip deeply affected Curtis.

"However," he said, "after spending eight weeks on a bus with a bunch of theater people, I never wanted to be around another actor for the rest of my life."

After graduating from high school, Curtis took a summer job on the assembly line at Fisher Body. In the fall, he enrolled at the University of Michigan in Flint. After his first semester, his grade point average was zero. He failed everything except for one class, in which he got a D. Then on September 15, 1972, at eighteen years of age, Curtis told his father that he was through with school and that he wanted to work in the factory and make money. Curtis said:

> My father's thought was, "OK. Come on in. Once you get a taste of this, you'll be back in school in no time at all." Had I taken care of business in school and done what I had to do and not been greedy, wanting to have a new car or stereo or music, then I wouldn't have been in the factory for as long as I was.

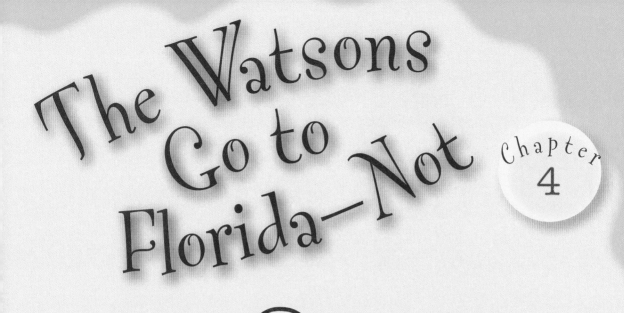

The Watsons Go to Florida—Not

During breaks at the factory, Curtis wrote about the things that bothered him, trying to escape the noise and the boredom. "It made me feel better," he said. "I'd go into a different world when I was writing."

In 1977, he and his wife settled in Windsor, Ontario, in Canada, about sixty miles from Flint. A year later, their son, Steven, was born. Then on September 25, 1985, Curtis left Fisher Body. For the next few years, he took low-paying jobs, including one as a campaign worker for a Democratic senator and another as a census taker. He also took night courses at the university.

25

Curtis in his high school graduation photo. After one year of college, he left to work at the Fisher Body plant.

In 1991, the Curtises' daughter, Cydney, was born. The following year, he entered a short-story contest and won. "In a lot of ways, that was the seed and the spark that got me going," he said. By then, Curtis was working as a clerk at a warehouse in the Detroit area. It was a tough job physically, using a hand truck with no power to unload computer paper off of fifty-three-foot trailers. Curtis also ordered all the lubricants for the company's machines and was the only one who could shut the place down. The company was happy with him, yet he was the lowest paid person there. Eventually, he applied for a job helping customers with questions and problems.

He said:

Normally I'd go to work in jeans and sweatshirts because I always got dirty, but on the day of the interview I brought a suit. The two women who interviewed me laughed and said that I didn't have to wear a suit. I told them that I was taking the job seriously and that I wanted them to take me seriously. Two weeks later, I was told I didn't get the job. They said they didn't think I was ready to talk to the public.

In 1993, Curtis took a year off from the warehouse to write. "With a clarity I don't ordinarily have, I told myself that this was an important opportunity," he said. "I had to take advantage of it and get something done. So I looked at it as a job." Curtis used the Windsor Public Library, a few miles from where he lived, as his office.

I usually went there six days a week. I'd be there when it opened at 8:00 A.M., and I'd stay for four or five hours. Eventually I drifted down to the children's section, not because I intended to write a children's book, but because homeless people who would come to the library and stay for the day did not go into the children's section. To get some privacy, that's where I'd read and work on *The Watsons Go to Florida—1963.*

The idea for the story came to Curtis during a car trip he and his family took to Florida, driving straight through for twenty-four hours, stopping only for gas and bathroom breaks—a trip similar to the one the Watsons made.

> I had written it up to the part where the boy meets his grandmother in Florida. Then the story stopped. I thought I had better set it aside and get a new project going—one with a better ending, or hopefully, something else would come of this one.

Around that time, Curtis submitted two pieces of his writing to a contest at the University of Michigan in Ann Arbor: an essay about working in the factory and the warehouse, and *The Watsons Go to Florida—1963* as a work in progress. His novel came in second place, and his essay won the Jules and Avery Hopwood Award.

Soon after that, Curtis's son Steven brought home a poem called *Ballad of Birmingham* by Dudley Randall. The poem is about the bombing of the 16th Street Baptist Church. "I can remember to this day

Christopher as a boy with Cydney and David in 1962. Many of the events in *The Watsons Go to Birmingham* are based on those from Curtis's childhood.

reading it at the kitchen table and thinking that I finally knew what was going to happen to the Watsons," said Curtis. "Then I went and changed the story."

Steven has always been his father's first reader. "He is perceptive and he has a good ear for what sounds right and true," said Curtis. "He felt some of the dialogue did not sound like what a kid would say."

Steven typed the revised manuscript into a borrowed computer, and Curtis sent *The Watsons Go to Birmingham—1963* to two publishing houses that were sponsoring writing contests. It did not win either contest; in fact, one editor thought that young readers would not like the story. However, Wendy Lamb, an editor at Random House, thought

Book FACT

The 16th Street Baptist Church Bombing

On September 15, 1963, four young girls—Addie Mae Collins, Denise McNair, Carole Robertson, and Cynthia Wesley—were killed when a bomb exploded at the 16th Street Baptist Church in Birmingham, Alabama. Twenty-two other people were injured. The bombing was an attack by members of the Ku Klux Klan, an organization of white racists. The tragedy was a turning point in the civil rights movement.

Christopher Paul Curtis

it would make a good novel for kids.

> If she had not shown a strong interest, I never would have sent it out again. I am the kind of person who doesn't take rejection very well. I take these things personally. I think you have to have a thick hide and be very driven to accept rejection and hang in there.

To this day, Curtis believes that things happen for a reason. He says that he often gets signals if things are going the right way. One day, after sending *The Watsons* to the writing contest, Curtis was driving home from work when an accident forced him to take a detour down a different street. He saw an old car for sale. "I love old cars," he said, "so I got out to look at it. It was a 1948 Plymouth—the same kind of car as the one I had written about in the story." Curtis believed this was a sign that everything would go well with the book.

The Watsons Go to Birmingham—1963 is a story about family and how family members help each other through troubled times. It also touches on the hurtful effects of racism. It is Curtis's most autobiographical book so far. In fact, Kenny Watson is a combination of Curtis and his brother David, and Kenny's sister, Joetta, is modeled after Curtis's sister Cydney.

When our mother and father were asleep, my older sister Lindsey used to sneak down to the kitchen and eat butter. She loved butter, and she would eat it by the spoonful. So I would see Lindsey going down and coming back with food and I thought I could do that, too. I remember crawling up onto the counter to get cookies from a shelf in a cabinet above the sink. When I looked down, there was my little sister Cydney looking up and saying, "I'm telling Mama." I was terrified. Just like Joetta, Cydney was a pest and a little goody-two-shoes.

Like Kenny, Curtis had a fascination with matches when he was about seven or eight.

> I would light matches, throw them in the toilet, and flush. My mother was scared to death that I would burn the house down. She warned me many times not to do it. She finally told me that if I lit another match in the house she would burn me. Of course, I got ahold of some matches again. I locked the bathroom door, but my mother broke in, grabbed me by the collar, threw me on the couch and said, "Don't you move," in the tone of voice that I knew she meant something. I was terrified. She went to the kitchen and came back with a book a matches, a Band-Aid, and jar of Vaseline. She told me to stick my finger out as she lit the matches, but my sister Cydney kept blowing them out. It is exactly like it happened in the story.

The in-car record player was real, too. Hoping to replace a car radio that had been stolen from his car, Curtis went to Duke's Tape Shack in Flint to get a new one. Duke's had an in-car record player. It was offered as an option on a 1957 Chrysler Imperial. "It was some of the worst technology ever developed because every time you went over a bump and every time you made a turn, it would scratch the record," he said. "Besides which, vinyl records melted in a hot car. But when I saw the in-car record player in the Tape Shack, I thought it would be interesting for the Watsons to have one."

The Watsons Go to Birmingham has been translated into thirteen different languages and is required reading for students all around the country. Curtis said it will always be special

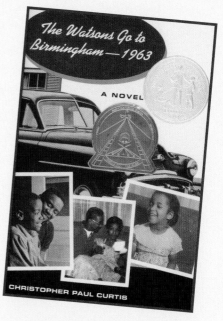

The Watsons Go to Birmingham—1963 won many awards.

to him. "It was my first book and I love the story," he said, "but it is also special because it is the book that took me out of warehouse and into doing something that I love."

Kenny, Bud, Elijah, Luther, Deza, and Mr. Chickee, Too

"I don't want to write just nice stories," said Curtis. "History is amazing, and there are things I want to bring out about the past in my books." To do this, Curtis imagined what it would be like for somebody to go through the civil rights movement, like Kenny in *The Watsons Go to Birmingham—1963*, or through the Great Depression, like Bud in *Bud, Not Buddy*, or through slavery, like Elijah in *Elijah of Buxton*.

When he first began to work on *Bud, Not Buddy*, Curtis did not plan to write about an orphan or about his grandfathers. He was actually considering a story about the sit-down strikes that took place in the 1930s at the Fisher Body plant. Around the same time, Curtis attended a family reunion.

> They were talking about my grandfather, Herman E. Curtis, and his band back in the 1930s called the Dusky Devastators of the Depression. I thought it was really interesting, so I took notes. I'd write a little about the sit-down strike, but it would seem kind of stale, so I'd recount the stories about my grandfather.

Eventually, the voice of ten-year old Bud Caldwell, an orphan in search of his father, emerged. Bud's "Rules and Things for a Having a Funner Life and Making a Better Liar Out of Yourself" help him cope with homelessness and racism during a troubled time in American history. Curtis modeled Herman E. Calloway, the stand-up bass player for the Dusky Devastators of the Depression, after his paternal grandfather, Herman E. Curtis. The character Lefty Lewis is based on Curtis's maternal grandfather, Earl "Lefty" Lewis.

After reading the story, Curtis's mother pointed out that the character of Miss Thomas resembled

Real Grandfathers

Curtis's paternal grandfather, Herman E. Curtis, was a chauffeur, a boat captain, a truck painter, a classically trained musician, and a big bandleader in the 1930s. His maternal grandfather, Earl "Lefty" Lewis, was one of just a few African-American baggage porters at the Grand Rapids train station. He was also a pitcher in the minors of the Negro Baseball League.

Mrs. Jones, a singer with his grandfather's band. Curtis said:

> Somehow or another, I must have heard something, or maybe I just made the whole thing up. I don't know. That's one of the scary things about creativity. There are so many things that come to you, and you don't know if you're being original or if you're channeling it.

Curtis set *Bucking the Sarge* in modern-day Flint. He knew that because of the subject matter, the main character, Luther, had to be older and more experienced than Kenny or Bud. On the other hand, he did not plan to write for a younger audience when he wrote *Mr. Chickee's Funny Money* and *Mr. Chickee's Messy Mission*. The humorous mysteries just turned out that way.

With *Elijah of Buxton*, Curtis tackled another historical subject, offering readers a different perspective on slavery. The story takes place in the first permanent black settlement in Canada, forty miles from Detroit. Eleven-year-old Elijah, the first child born into freedom in a community of runaway slaves, sets out to find the thief who stole money that Elijah's friend had been saving to buy his family's freedom. The quest takes Elijah to America, where he learns firsthand about the horrors of slavery. "I never had a story come as effortlessly and as quickly as this one did," Curtis said.

In *Deza Malone*, the upcoming sequel to *Bud, Not Buddy*, Curtis revisits the Great Depression and Hooverville, where Deza, her brother, and her mother await the return of Deza's father.

Curtis said that whatever he writes, the story and the characters have to be genuine and authentic. "That's what makes it successful," he said. "I want the story and the people in it to be real. There are no perfect people. All people are flawed. I think that should be revealed in my writing, too."

Chapter 6

Refuge

One day while he was speaking at a conference, Curtis was asked what college he had graduated from. He explained that he needed four credit hours of French, which he felt doomed to fail, to complete his degree in political science. An administrator from the University of Michigan who was in the audience asked Curtis to be the commencement speaker at the university's upcoming graduation ceremony. In return, the university let him take an exam on *Bud, Not Buddy*. Curtis passed and graduated in 1999.

By that time, Curtis had found a new place to work. With the success of *The Watsons*, patrons

Curtis with one of the model cars from his collection

at the Windsor Public Library were eager to meet the award-winning author. "Not that I minded," he said, "but I am basically a shy person. Still, for me, writing is a social thing, and I like having people around. I just don't want to talk all the time." The library in the University of Windsor turned out to be the perfect place for Curtis to watch people, do research, read books, and write.

> However, when I'm almost done with a book, and I need to finish it, I have to be alone. So I take a train from Windsor to Montreal, a twelve-hour ride. Then I'll stay in Montreal for three or four days, polish off the book, and take the train back.

39

Award-Winning Books

Christopher Paul Curtis's books have won many awards. Here are some of them:

Elijah of Buxton
- Newbery Honor Book, 2008
- Coretta Scott King Author Award, 2008
- Scott O'Dell Award for Historical Fiction, 2008

Mr. Chickee's Funny Money
- Parents' Choice Gold Award, 2005

Bucking the Sarge
- Golden Kite Award for Fiction, 2004
- American Library Association Best Books for Young Adults, 2004
- Publisher's Weekly Best Children's Book of the Year, 2004

Bud, Not Buddy
- Newbery Medal, 2000
- Coretta Scott King Author Award, 2000
- School Library Journal Best Book of the Year, 2000

The Watsons Go to Birmingham—1963
- Newbery Honor Book, 1996
- Coretta Scott King Author Honor Book, 1996
- American Library Association Best Book for Young Adults, 1996

Curtis is up at 5:00 A.M. every day, a routine he became accustomed to when he worked at the factory. He begins each workday by having breakfast at a nearby diner, checking the daily newspapers, and reading what he has written the day before. Then he settles in at the library until about 11:15. He plays basketball, has lunch, and returns to the library from 1:00 to 4:00 P.M. In the evening, after dinner, he often goes back to the library to do a few more hours of work.

He said:

Writing is like doing a physical activity. I get in shape and I fall out of shape. When I fall out of shape, I have to get back in shape before I can perform well. Once I'm into it, I know I have to sit there and write. If I'm fed up with my characters, I'll switch over to something else. I usually have two or three things going on at the same time. It's important that I keep working. A lot of time things will work themselves out while I do some other writing. When I'm really into it, I might break out laughing or crying.

Once Curtis knows a character and the character's voice, then the writing starts to sail.

"I am so happy when I get to the point where I don't have a lot of false leads or dead ends and the story takes off and flies," he said. "I layer one thing on and that leads me to more doors. I keep going through doors, and the next thing I know I've arrived somewhere."

Although Curtis never studied writing formally, he learned how to create a good story by reading books and watching movies, then analyzing them to learn what works. "I am very opinionated," he said, "which is why I don't like to read my own books. I am often too critical of them."

Curtis enjoys everything about the writing process, including starting with nothing and working all the way through. He never has a problem finding ideas. In fact, his problem is weeding ideas out. Curtis said he honestly believes that you can take anything and make a story out of it.

There are only a few things Curtis does not like about writing—waiting for reviews to come in and receiving the first letter from his editor after she has read a new manuscript. He said:

The letter may be fifteen pages. On the first page she says how wonderful it is and on the second page she says it's the greatest. Then on all the rest of the pages she says, let's do some things differently. Again, it's a form of rejection. When I get the letter, I'll open it but I won't read it for a couple of weeks. After the first time I read it, I couldn't tell you anything that I read. Then I go back and read it again. Then three or four times later, I am finally able to see her points.

Curtis believes that all writers have unique stories because each writer looks at things differently. "A writer is a filter in a lot of ways, and we each filter what we have seen and heard and what we know," he said. "Ultimately, everybody has his or her own story."

Christopher Paul Curtis signs books for his fans. He encourages young people to be patient and keep at it if they want to be writers.

Curtis wants young aspiring writers to understand that writing may not come easily and it may not come early. His advice is to be patient and to keep at it. "Writing is so much fun because the writer is powerful," he said. "A writer can look back in time and can create and destroy things. You can do whatever you want. You're in control." Curtis also tells young writers not to write for the sake of getting published. "That will be if it's supposed to be. You have to come for the love of writing and for the love of what it does to you. Writing has always been a refuge for me."

Books by Christopher Paul Curtis

Bucking the Sarge

Bud, Not Buddy

Elijah of Buxton

Mr. Chickee's Funny Money

Mr. Chickee's Messy Mission

The Watsons Go to Birmingham—1963

campaign worker—A person who helps a candidate get elected.

census taker—A government employee who gathers information about the population.

channeling—Transmitting a message.

flawed—Not perfect.

foreman—The leader of a work crew.

Ku Klux Klan—A secret organization that uses violence against African Americans, Jews, and members of other minority groups.

maternal—On the mother's side.

opinionated—Having strong thoughts and opinions.

paternal—On the father's side.

perceptive—Having the ability to see and understand.

picketing—Standing or marching outside a business or organization in order to protest or demand something.

racism—Prejudice or discrimination based on race.

racist—Prejudiced against people because of their race.

refuge—A protected place; a source of comfort and relief.

segregated—Separated by race.

Books

Bostrom, Kathleen Long. *Winning Authors: Profiles of the Newbery Medalists*. Westport, Conn.: Libraries Unlimited, 2003.

McElmeel, Sharron L. *Children's Authors and Illustrators Too Good to Miss: Biographical Sketches and Bibliographies*. Westport, Conn.: Libraries Unlimited, 2004.

Internet Addresses

Christopher Paul Curtis: Random House
<http://www.randomhouse.com/features/
  christopherpaulcurtis/index.htm>

Christopher Paul Curtis Biography: Scholastic, Inc.
<http://www2.scholastic.com/browse/contributor.
  jsp?id=3261>

Index